Who Is Oprah Winfrey?

by Barbara Kramer

illustrated by Dede Putra

Penguin Workshop

For Callie and Kinsey—BK

To my big sis—DP

PENGUIN WORKSHOP
An Imprint of Penguin Random House LLC, New York

Visit us online at www.penguinrandomhouse.com.

Library of Congress Cataloging-in-Publication Data is available upon request.

ISBN 9781524787509 (paperback)   10 9 8 7 6 5 4 3 2 1
ISBN 9781524787516 (library binding)   10 9 8 7 6 5 4 3 2 1

Contents

Who Is Oprah Winfrey?

As a young girl in the 1950s, Oprah Winfrey loved to tell stories. She lived outside the town of Kosciusko (say: kah-zee-ESS-ko) in central Mississippi on her grandparents' farm. No other children lived nearby, so the farm animals became Oprah's friends. She named the pigs and chickens and told them stories.

Some of her tales were made up. Others came from the Bible. Oprah's grandmother Hattie Mae Lee used the Bible to teach Oprah to read at an early age. Oprah was smart and memorized Bible verses easily. She soon began reciting them at her church.

The first time Oprah stood at the front of the church to recite Bible verses was on Easter Sunday in 1957. She was only three years old. She wore a dress her grandmother had made and the shiny shoes she saved for Sundays. The rest of the week she went barefoot. "Jesus rose on Easter Day, hallelujah, hallelujah," Oprah announced. She did not sound nervous at all.

"That child sure can talk," church members said. Some called her gifted. Oprah didn't understand that word, but she thought it meant she was special. She loved the attention and continued to recite Bible verses at her church on Sundays. As she got older, she spoke at other

churches. She recited longer passages from the Bible. Sometimes she recited poems or sermons written by famous ministers.

Oprah's talent for speaking led to a very successful television career. For twenty-five years,

The Oprah Winfrey Show was one of the most-watched talk shows in the United States. Today, Oprah is one of the richest, most powerful women in the world. She says it all began when she was three years old, reciting Bible verses at the front of her church.

CHAPTER 1
Farm Girl

Orpah Gail Winfrey was born in Kosciusko, Mississippi, on January 29, 1954. She was named Orpah after a woman in the Bible. But most people had trouble pronouncing her name. They kept switching the *r* and the *p*. They always seemed to call her *Oprah*, and the name stuck.

Oprah's mother, Vernita Lee, was eighteen years old when Oprah was born. Her father, Vernon Winfrey, was in the US Army. He didn't know he was going to be a father when he returned to the army base in Alabama. He found out months later when Vernita sent him a newspaper article announcing Oprah's birth.

There were not many job opportunities for Vernita in Kosciusko. Many African Americans at

Oprah and her mother

the time were leaving the southern United States and moving north. They were looking for better jobs and a better life there. They also wanted to escape the segregation of the South. Vernita decided to do the same. She moved to Milwaukee,

Wisconsin, leaving four-year-old Oprah with her grandmother. Vernita planned to send for Oprah after she got settled.

Even though Oprah's grandparents were poor, she always had clean clothes to wear and never went hungry. Her grandmother made Oprah's clothes. Most of their food came from what they raised on the farm.

Segregation

Until the mid-1960s, in the southern United States, there were laws that kept black people and white people apart. That system was known as segregation. Black children and white children could not attend the same schools. Black people could not eat at restaurants for white people, and they had to sit at the back of buses. They could not use the same restrooms or drinking fountains.

In 1954, the US Supreme Court made an important ruling in a case called *Brown v. Board of Education*. It said schools could no longer be segregated. But it took a while before black children and white children would actually attend the same schools. It wasn't until the Civil Rights Act of 1964 that all state and local segregation laws finally ended.

A happy mother and daughter on the steps of the Supreme Court building following the *Brown v. Board of Education* decision, 1954

There was always work to do, and Oprah was expected to help. One of her jobs was to feed the chickens. The house had no indoor plumbing—no bathroom or running water—so Oprah had to bring water from a nearby well for drinking and doing dishes. On Saturdays, she hauled water to be heated on the stove and poured into a tin tub for bathing.

Oprah was afraid of her grandfather Earless Lee. "I remember him always throwing things at me or trying to shoo me away with his cane," Oprah recalled. She stayed away from him as much as possible.

Like many people of that time, Hattie Mae believed in physical punishment. She thought it helped children learn to be good. She whipped Oprah often. "It would be called child abuse now," Oprah once said. But Oprah also had good memories of her grandmother. She liked working with Hattie Mae in the garden. Then they sat on the porch snapping green beans and shelling the peas they picked. It was Hattie Mae who taught Oprah to kneel and say her prayers every night.

Because of Hattie Mae's lessons at home, Oprah could already read and write when she started kindergarten. The other students were just learning the alphabet. Oprah wrote her teacher a note. "I do not think I belong here," it said. Her teacher and the principal agreed. Oprah was moved up to first grade.

I do not think I belong here

When Oprah was six, she went to Milwaukee to live with her mother. Vernita had another daughter named Patricia by then. The three of them lived in one room they rented from the owner of the house. Vernita's job as a maid left her little time or energy for her two daughters. She worked hard, but did not earn quite enough money. When Oprah was eight, Vernita sent her to live with her father in Tennessee.

Vernon Winfrey and his wife, Zelma, lived in the city of Nashville. They did not have any children of their own, and they welcomed Oprah into their home. Zelma helped Oprah learn multiplication. She also took Oprah to the library, where she was thrilled to get her first library card. She read books such as *Strawberry Girl* by Lois Lenski. Oprah wanted to be the character in whatever book she was reading. When she read about a girl named Katie John, Oprah painted freckles on her face to be like that character.

Oprah began reciting Bible verses at the church they attended, just as she had with her grandmother. Word about her talent spread, and she was invited to speak at other churches in the city. Some of Oprah's classmates didn't like the attention she got. They made fun of her, calling her "the Preacher." It made Oprah angry, but their teasing did not stop her from reciting at church.

CHAPTER 2
City Life

In 1963, when the school year ended, Oprah went back to Milwaukee for the summer. Oprah's mother had moved into a two-bedroom apartment. She had also given birth to a son named Jeffrey. Oprah, Patricia, and Jeffrey shared one bedroom.

At the end of the summer, Vernon Winfrey drove to Milwaukee to get Oprah. But her mother did not want her to leave. Oprah didn't want to disappoint her mother, so she stayed in Milwaukee. Vernon was upset, but there was nothing he could do. He did not have legal custody of his daughter.

Oprah began the new school year in Milwaukee. She liked school, but at home, she was lonely. Vernita worked long hours. Oprah spent much of  her time looking after her younger brother and sister. She also did a lot of reading and watched television. She liked shows about happy families, like *Leave It to Beaver*, and shows that made her laugh, such as *I Love Lucy*.

When Oprah was nine, an older cousin hurt her in her most private places. Over the next five years, the abuse happened other times with relatives, and again with a friend of the family. Oprah never told anyone. She didn't think anyone would believe her. Keeping such a big secret made her feel all alone. (Although Oprah didn't tell anyone at the time, today she says you should tell someone, and "if they don't believe you, you keep telling until somebody does." If you need more information on who to tell, please see our note on page 105.)

One of Oprah's middle-school teachers noticed that Oprah didn't act like the other students. In the lunchroom, they were noisy and rowdy. Oprah sat in a corner reading quietly. The teacher

believed Oprah would be happier at another school. He helped her get into Upward Bound, a program that taught low-income students the skills they needed to attend college.

Through Upward Bound, Oprah began classes at Nicolet High School. It was about twenty miles from where she lived. She took three different

city buses each morning to get to the wealthy neighborhood where the school was located. Almost all the students at Nicolet were white, but they were friendly to Oprah. She wondered if they really liked her or if they just thought it was cool to have an African American friend.

Some of the girls invited Oprah to their homes. After seeing how they lived, Oprah hated going back to her small, crowded apartment. She didn't have money to do things like going out for pizza with her friends, so she stole money from her mother's purse.

Oprah started getting into other trouble, too. One time she even ran away from home! Her mother didn't know what to do, so she asked Vernon Winfrey to come and get their daughter.

Vernon and Zelma were happy to have Oprah back with them. But they soon discovered that fourteen-year-old Oprah was keeping a big secret. She was pregnant. Soon after arriving in Nashville, Oprah gave birth to a baby boy. He was born too early and died a short time later. Oprah was sad, but also determined to try to change her life for the better.

Vernon also wanted Oprah to turn her life around and end her wild ways. He made her wash off her heavy makeup and get rid of her short, tight skirts. He set a time for her to be home at night. He also expected Oprah to work hard in school.

Oprah started tenth grade at East High School in Nashville in September 1968. She was one of the first black students to attend East High.

In addition to her schoolwork, Zelma and Vernon gave Oprah other assignments. She had to learn twenty new vocabulary words each week. She also had to read five books every two weeks and write reports on them.

Oprah's Inspirations

Oprah liked books about strong women who overcame big obstacles. She read about Helen Keller, Harriet Tubman, and Sojourner Truth. When Oprah was sixteen, she read *I Know Why the Caged Bird Sings* by Maya Angelou. It is a true story about the author's life. Like Oprah, Maya had lived with her grandmother in the South for a while. Then she lived with her mother and, later, her father. Maya had also been abused by a man when she was just a young girl.

Oprah couldn't believe that someone had a life so similar to her own. She read the book over and over. It made her feel that she was not alone. As adults, Oprah and Maya became friends. Oprah said Maya had become like a mother to her.

Maya Angelou

Oprah had plenty of time to read because her father limited her to only one hour of watching television each day. Vernon was strict, but Oprah said it was what she needed.

CHAPTER 3
New Opportunities

In high school, Oprah became an honor student. She joined a club for public speaking, and continued to recite Bible verses, poems, and sermons at churches all around Nashville. In 1971, Oprah and another student were chosen to represent the state of Tennessee at the White House Conference on Youth. They were picked because they were strong students and good leaders. The conference was held in Colorado.

When Oprah returned home, she was interviewed by John Heidelberg on Nashville's WVOL radio station. He later asked Oprah if she would

John Heidelberg

represent the station in Nashville's Miss Fire Prevention beauty pageant. Oprah did not see herself as beautiful, but she thought it might be fun. "All you had to do was walk, parade around in an evening gown, answer some questions about your life," she recalled.

One of those questions was about future career plans. The other contestants said they wanted to be nurses or teachers. Oprah had not thought much about what she wanted to do, but she remembered seeing Barbara Walters reporting on the *Today* show that morning. So she told the judges she wanted to be a broadcast journalist, reporting the news on radio and television.

Oprah won the pageant. She was the first African American named Miss Fire Prevention in Nashville. Later, she went to the radio station to collect her prizes—a wristwatch and a digital clock.

While she was there, John Heidelberg asked if

she wanted to hear how her voice sounded recorded on tape. Oprah read the news story he handed her. She had been speaking in public since she was three years old. With all that experience, she sounded like a real reporter! Later, John played the tape for the station manager. The station manager offered Oprah a job at WVOL. She was seventeen years old and still in high school when she started working at the radio station. She read the news on the radio after school and on the weekends.

Oprah graduated from high school in June 1971. That fall, she enrolled at Tennessee State University. She paid for her classes with a scholarship she had won for a speech she gave in a contest. She continued to live at home and to work at the radio station.

In college, Oprah studied speech and drama. By that time, she was dreaming of becoming an actress. Because of her work schedule, she did not have time to perform in college plays. Instead, she memorized poems and passages from books and acted them out on her own. Oprah also continued to enter beauty pageants. She was named Miss Black Nashville and Miss Black Tennessee.

In 1973, a local TV station invited Oprah to audition for a job as co-anchor (news presenter) of the evening news. She didn't know how a TV news anchor should act. For the audition, she pretended she was Barbara Walters. She sat like Barbara, and looked into the camera as she had seen Barbara do. Her plan worked! Oprah became the first black television news anchor in Nashville—and the first female one as well. At nineteen, she was also the youngest newscaster to work in the city.

Oprah became an anchor at Nashville's station WLAC-TV, 1973.

In 1975, Oprah did not graduate with the rest of her college classmates. She quit school just one class short of getting her degree. Her father had always told her that education was the key to success, but Oprah was not worried about that. She already had a good job. In 1976, she got an even better offer from WJZ-TV in Baltimore, Maryland.

The job as a reporter and news anchor in Baltimore was a step up in Oprah's career. Baltimore had a bigger market. That meant a larger audience. Oprah also felt like it was time for her to move out of her father's house. After all, she was twenty-two years old and still living at home under her father's strict rules. She accepted the job and moved to Maryland.

Barbara Walters

Barbara Walters was born in 1929 in Boston, Massachusetts. She attended Sarah Lawrence College and, immediately after graduation, moved to New York City. In 1962, she began working as a reporter on NBC's *Today* show. Twelve years later, she became the first woman to cohost that show.

In 1976, Barbara was hired by ABC, becoming the first woman to co-anchor a national news show. She also began a series of *Barbara Walters Specials*. For those shows, she interviewed famous stars and world leaders. She was known for her outstanding interview skills and popularity with viewers.

In 1979, Barbara became a regular reporter on ABC's *20/20* news program. In 1997, she created *The View*, a daytime talk show. She was a cohost on the show until she retired from television in 2014.

CHAPTER 4
Hard Times in Baltimore

One of the best things that happened to Oprah in Baltimore was meeting Gayle King, a production assistant at the station. Gayle worked behind the scenes to help get shows ready to air.

At first, Oprah and Gayle did not know each other very well. That changed one day when the city got hit with a big snowstorm. Oprah knew Gayle had a long drive home, and invited her to stay overnight at her apartment. That night they stayed up late talking about everything, including their jobs at the station. They have been best friends ever since.

Gayle King

Gayle King was born on December 28, 1954, in Chevy Chase, Maryland. She spent part of her childhood in the country of Turkey, where her father was stationed for his job with the US government. She graduated from the University of Maryland in 1976 and began her television career. In 1978, she moved to Kansas City, Missouri, for a job as a news anchor. Four years later, Gayle returned to the East Coast to work as a news anchor in Hartford, Connecticut, for eighteen years.

Gayle became an editor of *O, the Oprah Magazine* in 1999. She was also a special correspondent for *The Oprah Winfrey Show*. In 2011, she became cohost of the news program *CBS This Morning*. That same year, she also began hosting *The Gayle King Show* on the OWN television network.

Unfortunately, things were not going so well for Oprah at work. She was used to just being herself when she read the news. If she made a mistake, such as saying a word wrong, she laughed. News anchors were expected to read the news without showing their feelings. But Oprah was not afraid to show her emotions on the air.

Once, when she had to interview a woman who had lost her children in a house fire, Oprah cried.

And you could tell if a story made her angry.

The station managers wanted Oprah to be more professional. They also decided she needed a makeover. They sent her to a fancy hair salon in New York City. The stylist did a special treatment on Oprah's hair and left it on too long. It did so much damage that all her hair fell out. "I had two little spriggles, like a bald man," Oprah said. She wore scarves to cover her head while her hair grew back.

Until her job in Baltimore, success had come easily to Oprah. Now she was taken off the evening news. She began doing short reports for the morning news. It was a step down from being a news anchor. Oprah was embarrassed, and she

worried that she might lose her job. After work, she began hanging out at the food court in the mall across the street from her apartment. She hoped food would somehow make her feel better. But it only made her gain weight.

Other men and women who worked as news reporters were slim and attractive. It was considered part of the job to be pretty. Oprah had never worried about her weight before. But now she was concerned. Over time, she gained even more weight.

Things at work improved for Oprah when a new station manager arrived. He saw something in Oprah. She was warm and friendly. She was the type of person he wanted for a morning talk show he was starting called *People Are Talking*. He asked Oprah to cohost the show with Richard Sher.

Talking with guests on the show was easy for Oprah. "This is what I was born to do," she said after the first show. "This is like breathing."

People Are Talking had big competition. It was on television at the same time as *The Phil Donahue Show*. That show aired across the entire country. It was the highest-rated talk show in the nation. Ratings are important in television. High ratings mean more people are watching.

Phil Donahue

Companies like to advertise on shows viewed by the most people. Those advertising dollars are how television stations make money. *People Are Talking* was a success from the start. Within a month it was beating *The Phil Donahue Show* in ratings for the Baltimore area!

Oprah cohosted *People Are Talking* for five years. Then a friend told her about a job opening at WLS-TV in Chicago. They were looking for a host for *A.M. Chicago*, a morning talk show. Oprah liked the idea because she would be hosting her own show rather than being a cohost. But her friends and coworkers said she was making a mistake. They said she wasn't right for the job because she was not like most other talk-show hosts.

At that time, most hosts were white men. Oprah was a black woman who was slightly overweight. But she had a good feeling about Chicago. She believed it was where she was meant to be.

CHAPTER 5
Welcome to Chicago

Oprah hosted *A.M. Chicago* for the first time on January 2, 1984. Once again, the show was on at the same time as *The Phil Donahue Show*. The station manager told Oprah not to worry. "Just go on the air and be yourself," he said.

And that's what Oprah did. Soon she was beating *The Phil Donahue Show* in ratings in the Chicago area. By 1985, *A.M. Chicago* expanded from thirty minutes to a full hour. And—best of all—the name was changed to *The Oprah Winfrey Show*.

People liked the way Oprah really listened to what her guests had to say. As a talk-show host, she did not need to hide her feelings. She sometimes had tears in her eyes when a guest talked about something sad. Oprah also shared stories about herself, including her feelings about gaining weight, and she laughed easily. Viewers felt like they were spending time with a good friend.

Oprah did not live far from the studio where she hosted her show. On nice days, she liked to walk to work. As she became more popular, that got harder. People stopped her to give her a hug or ask for an autograph. Sometimes they wanted to have their picture taken with her. One time a woman bus driver pulled over, got out of the bus, and ran over to shake Oprah's hand. The bus was full of passengers. Instead of being upset by the delay, they clapped!

Oprah soon got a new opportunity when music and movie producer Quincy Jones came to Chicago on business. Jones was working on

Quincy Jones

making the book *The Color Purple* into a movie. One morning he turned on the TV in his Chicago hotel room and saw Oprah hosting her show. "That's Sofia!" he said. Sofia is a character from the book. Jones contacted Oprah about doing an audition with Steven Spielberg, the director of the movie.

Oprah had read the book when it first came out. She *really* wanted to play the part of Sofia. Oprah was offered the role, but there was a problem. The movie would be filmed in North Carolina and California. Oprah could not be in another state working on a movie and still do her show in Chicago. Fortunately, she never had to choose between the movie and her show. The station managers did not want to lose their popular star. They gave Oprah three months off to work on the movie. While she was gone, the station filled in with guest hosts and reruns.

Oprah playing Sofia in *The Color Purple*

The Color Purple

The Color Purple, a book written by Alice Walker, was published in 1982. The main character, Celie, is an uneducated black woman in the 1930s who  begins writing letters to God. In those letters, she pours out her feelings about the physical abuse and hardships she has suffered in her life. Gradually, she learns to stand up for herself.

In 1983, *The Color Purple* won two very important book awards—the Pulitzer Prize for fiction and the National Book Award. But a lot of people were not ready to talk about abuse. The book was banned in many school and public libraries.

The Color Purple was released in December 1985. Movie critics praised Oprah for her role as Sofia. In 1986, she was nominated for an Academy Award for best supporting actress! She didn't win, but being nominated for her first movie role was a big honor.

Oprah attends the Academy Awards, 1986.

There was also an exciting change coming to *The Oprah Winfrey Show*. Until then, it had aired only in Chicago. But it would soon be syndicated. That meant the show would air on television channels in cities across the United States. It made Oprah the first African American woman to host her own talk show on national TV.

The first day of syndication was September 8, 1986. The show was seen on over one hundred stations across the country. Oprah earned money from each of those stations and quickly became a very rich woman. At thirty-two, she was already a multimillionaire. And she was just getting started.

CHAPTER 6
Soaring Higher

In 1986, Oprah appeared in another movie, *Native Son*. It seemed that she was on her way to achieving her college dream of being an actress. But by that time, she had even bigger dreams. It was not enough to act in movies. She wanted to produce—to be in charge of making them.

In 1986, she formed her own company, Harpo Productions. *Harpo* is *Oprah* spelled backward. She began looking for interesting books and strong stories about African American women to make into movies.

Oprah was enjoying her success, but it

bothered her that she had never finished college. Her father still asked her when she was going to get her degree every time she spoke to him. In 1987, she did a special project for Tennessee State University to finally earn her diploma. In May, she was the speaker at her own graduation!

During her speech, Oprah announced that she was setting up a scholarship program at the college in her father's name. The scholarships would go to bright students who did not have enough money to pay for college.

That year, Oprah won a Daytime Emmy Award for outstanding talk-show host. The Emmys honor the best in television. Oprah had a lot to be happy about, including a new man in her life, Stedman Graham.

Daytime Emmy Award

Oprah and Stedman had seen each other at events around town. They talked, but they did not start dating until about two years after they first met. Oprah was not in a hurry to start a relationship. In the past, she'd had a habit of dating men who were not quite right for her. Oprah knew from their very first date that Stedman was different. He was kind, and he listened to what she had to say.

Stedman Graham

Stedman Graham

Stedman Graham was born in New Jersey in 1951. He is an author, educator, and businessman. Two of his eleven books, including *You Can Make It Happen: A Nine-Step Plan for Success*, have become *New York Times* Best Sellers. He is also a public speaker who specializes in teaching people ways to overcome obstacles in their lives. In 2008, Stedman founded the My Life Is About Foundation, a nonprofit organization to help teenagers learn ways to achieve their dreams. Stedman was married at one time and has a daughter named Wendy.

Oprah continued to work on her show. She was also building her company. In 1988, Harpo Productions became the owner of *The Oprah Winfrey Show*. Because the TV station no longer owned her show, Oprah had more control over the hours she worked. The shows were taped in front of an audience, but viewers at home saw them later. Each week, Oprah taped two shows on Monday and Tuesday and one show on Wednesday. That left the rest of the week for other projects, such as making movies.

Oprah's next step was finding a new studio space. She spent $10 million to buy a building on Chicago's West Side. It covered almost a whole city block. She spent another $10 million making changes to the building. When the work was finished, Harpo Studios had space for filming *The Oprah Winfrey Show* and studios for making movies. There were also offices, and a gym and a cafeteria for the people who worked there.

With the opening of Harpo Studios, Oprah became the first African American woman to own her own production studio. She was only the third American woman to do so. The first two were Mary Pickford and Lucille Ball.

Mary Pickford

Lucille Ball

One of the very first projects for Harpo Productions was a television miniseries called *The Women of Brewster Place*. That story—about seven women who live in the same apartment building—was based on a book by Gloria Naylor.

Cast of *The Women of Brewster Place*

Oprah starred as Mattie Michael, one of the women.

The miniseries was a success, but a later attempt to turn it into a weekly television series did not work out as well. It was canceled after only a few episodes. According to some reports, Oprah lost $10 million on the project. But she knew that along with success, there was always a chance of failure. And Oprah had many successes, providing her a lifestyle that others could only imagine.

CHAPTER 7
Making Changes

Oprah lived in an apartment that covered the fifty-seventh floor of a high-rise building. From her windows, she had a view of the city of Chicago and the sailboats on Lake Michigan. When she wanted to get away from the city, she went to her 160-acre farm in Indiana. Oprah's Indiana property had a large home and an eight-room guesthouse. There was also a pool, a gym, a tennis court, and a barn where Oprah kept nine horses.

At the farm, Oprah read and relaxed. She worked in her garden and walked the dogs she had adopted. At one time, she had as many as eleven dogs. Nine of them stayed on the farm. Her two cocker spaniels, Solomon and Sophie, went everywhere with her, including work.

Sophie and Solomon

In June 1992, Oprah won her third Daytime Emmy Award for outstanding talk-show host. It should have been a happy time, but Oprah could not enjoy it. Ever since her days in Baltimore, she had struggled with her weight. She sometimes lost weight and then gained it back. At the time of the awards show, she was uncomfortable in her dress. She did not want to walk up to the stage to accept the award.

After the Emmy Awards show, Oprah went to a spa in Colorado. She spent three weeks there hiking, running, and eating healthy meals. She lost twelve pounds and wanted to continue her healthy new lifestyle.

Back in Chicago, Oprah hired a personal chef to prepare low-fat meals. She also worked with a personal trainer. He started her out slowly, with a walking program. She soon started jogging, working up to eight miles a day. After sixteen months, she had lost about eighty-five pounds and was feeling healthier.

As Oprah concentrated on her own goals, some people began to wonder about her relationship with Stedman. In 1992, they had announced their engagement. They set a wedding date for the following year. That day came and went, but there was no wedding. People said it was because Oprah and Stedman had problems in their relationship. Some made up stories about what those problems were. This was the downside to being famous.

Oprah was frustrated that people said and wrote things that were not true about her and the people in her life. She said there were no problems in her relationship with Stedman. They were happy together, but they both had busy careers. There had been no time to plan a wedding.

One thing Oprah was busy with was making

changes to her show. Some talk shows had guests who argued and yelled at each other. Sometimes that led to fights on national television. Those shows got high ratings. People watched just to see what might happen.

Oprah admitted that she had hosted some shows where guests argued and said hurtful things to each other. She regretted that, and she vowed to change the direction of her show. Beginning in 1994, she focused on using her show to help others. She invited experts to give advice about money, relationships, and health and fitness. Oprah planned shows about people who had overcome great obstacles in their lives, and about everyday people who had acted as heroes. And, because friends are so important to Oprah, there were single shows that were just about friendship. She speaks to her best friend, Gayle King, by phone almost every night.

Not everyone liked the new direction of *The Oprah Winfrey Show*. Some thought Oprah was telling people how to live their lives. Ratings for the show went down a bit, but they soon rose again. *The Oprah Winfrey Show* remained number one in ratings among talk shows, and Oprah continued to make whatever changes she thought were best.

CHAPTER 8
Helping Others

Reading has always been important to Oprah. She wanted to share that love with others, so in 1996, she started Oprah's Book Club. Oprah picked a book to be featured on her talk show. She waited one month for people to read it. Then an entire show would be spent talking about the book. Oprah's audience members were people who had read the book. Most times, the author would make a guest appearance on the show as well.

Oprah with Toni Morrison, author of *Song of Solomon*

Sales soared for every book Oprah selected for her book club. Most of the books she picked sold more than a million copies. Oprah was very excited about the letters she got from her viewers. Some said they had not read a book in years. Now they were reading again and loving it.

Oprah also challenged her viewers to help others. She had given millions of dollars to libraries, colleges, and programs to help children. She provided college scholarships to students in need. She also made it possible for low-income students to go to prep schools to better prepare

them for college—the way Upward Bound had helped her.

Oprah was able to make large donations to charities, but she knew even small amounts could make a difference. In 1998, she created Oprah's Angel Network, and invited her fans to send their pocket change. The money went into what became known as "the World's Largest Piggy Bank."

The Angel Network raised more than $3.5 million in the first year alone! Over the next three years, 150 young people received scholarships through that program. Each was worth $25,000. Money from the Angel Network has also gone to Habitat for Humanity. Through that program, volunteers help build homes for people who cannot afford them. The Angel Network also supported women's shelters, built youth shelters, and established schools in countries around the world.

Because she was so kind, people trusted

Oprah. They really listened to what she had to say. In 1996, Oprah did a show that included a discussion of dangerous foods. One of the guests on that show spoke about mad cow disease and how brain disease in cattle could spread to people who ate meat from infected cows. During the show, Oprah said, "It has just stopped me cold from eating another burger."

After that show, sales of beef went down, and cattle ranchers in Texas blamed Oprah. In 1997, the Texas Beef Group filed a lawsuit against her, asking for over $10 million. It would have been easy for Oprah to just pay them, but she didn't. She believed she had a right to do shows on important topics such as mad cow disease. She was willing to fight for that right in court.

Oprah Winfrey arrives in Texas for 'beef libel' trial

In January 1998, the trial started in Amarillo, Texas. It lasted six weeks. During that time, Oprah continued to host her show. She spent her days in court. After a dinner break, she filmed her show in the evenings in the Amarillo Little Theatre.

On February 26, the court ruled that Oprah was not responsible for beef sales going down. Outside the courtroom, Oprah celebrated. She pumped her fists into the air and said, "Free speech not only lives, it rocks!"

"You Get a Car!"

Oprah gives millions of dollars to charity. She also likes to surprise her family, friends, and staff members with gifts. And she is famous for being very generous to the studio audience of her talk show.

On September 13, 2004, Oprah announced that one lucky person would get the keys to a brand-new Pontiac G6. Then she surprised the audience by giving them all a new car. She excitedly pointed to audience members, shouting, "You get a car!" and "You get a car!" The crowd screamed with joy.

About the "You get a car!" moment, Oprah remembered it as "one of my all-time favorite happiest moments ever."

By 1998, Oprah had won seven Daytime
Emmy Awards for best talk-show host. That year,
she received an Emmy for Lifetime Achievement.
Barbara Walters presented the award to Oprah,

praising her for the way she helped others. "The only thing greater than Oprah's accomplishments is the size of her heart," Barbara said.

Along with doing her talk show, Oprah was busy making movies. She had an agreement with the ABC television network to do a series of six made-for-television movies. Oprah also made a feature film based on a book she loved. *Beloved,* written by award-winning author Toni Morrison, is the story of a former slave who is haunted by her past. Oprah starred in the movie, playing the role of Sethe, the former slave.

Beloved was released in theaters in October 1998. Movie critics had good things to say

about the acting, especially Oprah's. But they also said the three-hour movie was too long and that the story was confusing. Ticket sales were low. Oprah believed it was an important story. She was upset that people did not turn out to see it. *Beloved*'s lack of success was one of Oprah's biggest disappointments. But—as always—she didn't give up. She moved on to new and bigger projects.

CHAPTER 9
New Directions

In 2000, Oprah entered the world of publishing and created *O, the Oprah Magazine.*

First issue of *O, the Oprah Magazine*

It expanded on the ideas Oprah discussed on her show and brought them to an even bigger audience. Women who could not get enough of Oprah now had a magazine. Oprah was reaching more people than ever with her message about helping others live their best lives.

It can take a few years for a new magazine to find readers. *O, the Oprah Magazine* was a success from the start. Within months, there were

1.9 million subscribers. Oprah named her best friend, Gayle King, editor-at-large for the magazine. Gayle reports to Oprah, who makes final decisions about what articles to include each month. Oprah is on the cover of every issue.

Oprah had come a long way from the barefoot young girl on a farm in Mississippi. But she had never lost her love for the land. In 2001, she bought a forty-two-acre estate in Montecito,

Oprah estate in Montecito, California

California. From her home, she had a view of the ocean. She added a forest of oak trees, a fountain, and a large garden. In 2002, she bought property in Hawaii. She grows fruits and vegetables there, too. Oprah says that some of her happiest times are harvest days. She still likes growing the food she eats.

Oprah also continued to look for ways to help others. In 2002, she traveled to South Africa to give toys, books, school supplies, and clothes to fifty thousand children. For most of the children, it was the first time they had ever received a gift. On that trip, Oprah announced her plan to build the Oprah Winfrey Leadership Academy for Girls. The boarding school would be built in a village about an hour's drive from the city of Johannesburg.

Oprah was involved with every step of the planning, including how the dorm rooms were decorated. She also helped select the students

Oprah visits schoolchildren in South Africa, 2002.

who would live and study at the school. They were chosen because of need and ability, and for their leadership qualities. Oprah wanted students who would use their education to make South Africa a better country. After five years of work, the school opened in 2007.

For Oprah, the young women at the school are family. She had often thought about having children, but there never seemed to be a good time.

In 2009, Oprah announced that *The Oprah Winfrey Show* would end with the 2010–2011 season. Ending the show was a difficult decision, but Oprah felt the time was right. "This show has been my life," she said, "and I love it enough to know when it's time to say goodbye." The last episode aired on May 25, 2011, after twenty-five seasons. But Oprah had no plans to slow down. She had already partnered with Discovery Communications to create a new television network called OWN (the Oprah Winfrey Network). It had begun broadcasting on January 1, 2011.

OPRAH WINFREY NETWORK

OWN got off to a slow start, and Oprah was discouraged. "I didn't expect failure," she said. "I was tested and I had to dig deep."

As always, Stedman was by Oprah's side. They had been together for twenty-five years. Oprah said they were happy together, but they no longer talked about marriage. "It works so well the way it is, I wouldn't want to mess it up," she explained.

Stedman encouraged Oprah. He knew she could make OWN successful. She just needed to do the work.

Oprah decided to change the type of shows on the OWN network. She wanted to continue to produce talk shows hosted by experts. But people wanted a bigger variety of programs. For that, Oprah teamed up with actor and writer Tyler Perry. One of the series he created, *The Haves and the Have Nots*, quickly became a hit.

Cast of *The Haves and the Have Nots*

Tyler Perry

Tyler Perry was born in New Orleans, Louisiana, in 1969. He was close to his mother. But his father was physically abusive, and Tyler grew into an unhappy teenager. In 1991, he was working in an office when he saw an episode of *The Oprah Winfrey Show* that changed his life. On that show, Oprah talked about journaling and how important it is to write about your feelings, both good and bad.

Tyler began writing letters to himself. Those letters led to his first play, *I Know I've Been Changed*. In 2000, his play *I Can Do Bad All by Myself* introduced a character named Madea. That tough and funny woman was based on Tyler's mother. Madea made her movie debut in *Diary of a Mad Black Woman* in 2005. Other Madea films have followed, with Tyler, dressed as a woman, in the starring role. Today Tyler is a writer, producer, and actor onstage, in film, and on television.

Tyler Perry as Madea

While Oprah worked to get OWN off the ground, she also returned to acting. It had been fifteen years since she starred in *Beloved*. She had not acted in another movie since then. In 2013, she returned to the big screen in *Lee Daniels' The Butler*. It was loosely based on the true story of Eugene Allen. He had served as a White House butler for eight presidents. Forest Whitaker played Cecil Gaines, a fictional character based on Eugene. Oprah costarred as his wife, Gloria.

Eugene Allen with President Ronald Reagan and his wife, Nancy

Oprah receives the Presidential Medal of Freedom.

In the fall of 2013, Oprah received the Presidential Medal of Freedom. It is the highest honor given to a US civilian, someone who is not in the military. President Barack Obama presented the award to Oprah for her work as a broadcast journalist and for all she had done to help others.

Oprah followed *Lee Daniels' The Butler* with *Selma*, released in 2014. That film was based on the true story of the civil rights marches from Selma, Alabama, to the state's capital city, Montgomery, in 1965. Many African Americans had been kept from registering, or signing up, to vote in elections

Selma to Montgomery march, 1965

because of unfair rules. The marches, led by Dr. Martin Luther King Jr., were a protest against those rules. Oprah was a producer of the movie. She also played the role of Annie Lee Cooper, a woman who tried to register to vote several times. Each time she was turned away.

The following year, Oprah ended an important chapter in her life. The offices for OWN were in West Hollywood, California. But Oprah still had an apartment and Harpo Studios in Chicago. She wanted everything to be in one place, so she put the Chicago properties up for sale. By the end of 2015, she had moved Harpo Studios to California.

By that time, Oprah had turned much of the day-to-day work of running her network over to longtime employees whom she trusted. That gave her time to explore even more new opportunities.

CHAPTER 10
The Master of Media

In 2015, Oprah invested in a company called Weight Watchers International, Inc. When she was very busy or stressed, she sometimes got away from eating healthy foods and exercising. Then she gained weight. Once again, she was trying to lose weight, so she tried the Weight Watchers program. After losing fourteen pounds, she decided the program worked and the company was a good investment. She bought 10 percent of the company.

The year 2017 was a busy one for Oprah. In January, her cookbook, *Food, Health, and Happiness*, was released. She worked with some of her favorite chefs to create the recipes. In addition, she shared family photos and stories about her life.

Oprah also worked with a team of chefs to create her own line of foods called O, That's Good!—packaged foods that include soups and side dishes. Ten percent of the profits from O, That's Good! go to the charities Rise Against Hunger and Feeding America. That fall, she began work as a special reporter on the evening news program *60 Minutes*.

Oprah continues to produce and act in movies, such as *The Immortal Life of Henrietta Lacks*. She traveled to New Zealand to film her role as Mrs. Which, a wise guide, in *A Wrinkle in Time*, based on the popular book written by Madeleine L'Engle.

In 2018, Oprah was honored at the Golden Globes award ceremony, where she received the Cecil B. DeMille Award. Named for the famous filmmaker, it is given annually to someone who has made "outstanding contributions to the world of entertainment." Oprah was the first African American woman to receive that honor.

What most people remembered from that night was Oprah's powerful acceptance speech. She received several standing ovations as she talked about how important it is to speak up when people in power are hurting you. "Speaking your truth is the most powerful tool we all have," she said.

By the next morning, the Internet was buzzing with exciting headlines: "Oprah for President!" Oprah may not be 100 percent qualified to be president, but many people hoped she would run for office. It showed just how strongly people believe in, and trust, Oprah.

As a young girl, Oprah told stories to the pigs and chickens on her grandparents' farm. Now her voice is heard around the world. She is a giant in the entertainment business and she has done it all: She has been the star of her own television show, an actress, and a movie producer. She is also a writer, a magazine publisher, and the owner of her own television network. She is sometimes called the Master of Media.

Her hard work has made her one of the richest, most powerful women in the world. But Oprah is best known for the ways she continues to help and encourage others. To those who have watched her television show, read her magazine, and welcomed her advice, Oprah remains a trusted and true friend.

Oprah has said, "What stops the cycle of abuse is awareness." In 1991, she testified before a committee in the US Senate, sharing her painful story about being abused as a child. She wanted Congress to create a national registry of child abusers. The National Child Protection Act, also known as "the Oprah Bill," was signed into law by President Bill Clinton in 1993. According to the law, each state is required to report child abuse crime information to the national registry.

If you, or someone you know, need confidential support or need to report abuse, talk to a trusted adult, such as a teacher, guidance counselor, coach, or parent. You can also call the National Sexual Assault Hotline at 1-800-656-HOPE (4673). You can contact a counselor at Childhelp at 1-800-422-4453 or Kids Help Phone at 1-800-668-6868.

Timeline of Oprah Winfrey's Life

1954	Born in Kosciusko, Mississippi, on January 29
1960	Moves to Milwaukee, Wisconsin, to live with her mother
1968	Moves to Nashville, Tennessee, to live with her father
1971	Begins reading the news at WVOL
	Enrolls at Tennessee State University
1973	Becomes co-anchor of the weekend news at WLAC-TV
1976	Becomes a reporter and news anchor at WJZ-TV
1978	Begins cohosting *People Are Talking*
1984	Begins hosting *A.M. Chicago*
1985	*A.M. Chicago* becomes *The Oprah Winfrey Show*
	Makes her first movie appearance in *The Color Purple*
1986	*The Oprah Winfrey Show* is syndicated
	Founds Harpo Productions
1996	Launches Oprah's Book Club
1998	Creates Oprah's Angel Network
2000	Begins publishing *O, the Oprah Magazine*
2007	Opens the Oprah Winfrey Leadership Academy for Girls in South Africa
2011	Founds the OWN channel
2013	Stars in *Lee Daniels' The Butler*, her first movie role in fifteen years
2018	Stars in *A Wrinkle in Time*

Timeline of the World

1951 — First episode of *I Love Lucy* is televised

1954 — The Tournament of Roses Parade becomes the first event televised nationally in color

1963 — Dr. Martin Luther King Jr. delivers his "I Have a Dream" speech before two hundred thousand people in Washington, DC

1964 — The Civil Rights Act is signed into law, making segregation illegal in the United States

1968 — Shirley Chisholm becomes the first black woman elected to the US Congress

1970 — First Earth Day is celebrated

1973 — Skylab, the first US space station, is launched

1981 — MTV begins airing music videos

1985 — About forty-five popular singers unite to record the song "We Are the World" to raise money to fight hunger in Africa

1994 — Nelson Mandela is elected the first black president of South Africa

2001 — Terrorists attack the World Trade Center in New York City and the Pentagon building in Washington, DC

2008 — Barack Obama is elected the first African American president of the United States

2016 — Chicago Cubs win their first World Series since 1908

Bibliography

*Books for young readers

*Cooper, Ilene. *Up Close: Oprah Winfrey.* New York: Puffin, 2008.

*Dakers, Diane. *Oprah Winfrey: Media Legend and Inspiration to Millions.* New York: Crabtree Publishing Company, 2016.

*Krohn, Katherine E. *Oprah Winfrey.* Minneapolis: Lerner Publications Company, 2002.

*Lies, Anne. *Oprah Winfrey: Media Mogul.* Edina, MN: ABDO Publishing Company, 2011.

Lowe, Janet. *Oprah Winfrey Speaks: Insight from the World's Most Influential Voice.* New York: John Wiley & Sons, 1998.

*Paprocki, Sherry Beck. *Oprah Winfrey: Talk Show Host and Media Magnate.* New York: Chelsea House Publishers, 2006.

Winfrey, Oprah. *What I Know for Sure.* New York: Flatiron Books, 2014.

Winfrey, Oprah, with Lisa Kogan. *Food, Health, and Happiness: 115 On-Point Recipes for Great Meals and a Better Life.* New York: Flatiron Books, 2017.

Websites

www.achievement.org/achiever/oprah-winfrey/#interview

www.biography.com/people/oprah-winfrey-9534419

www.imdb.com/name/nm0001856/bio

www.oprah.com